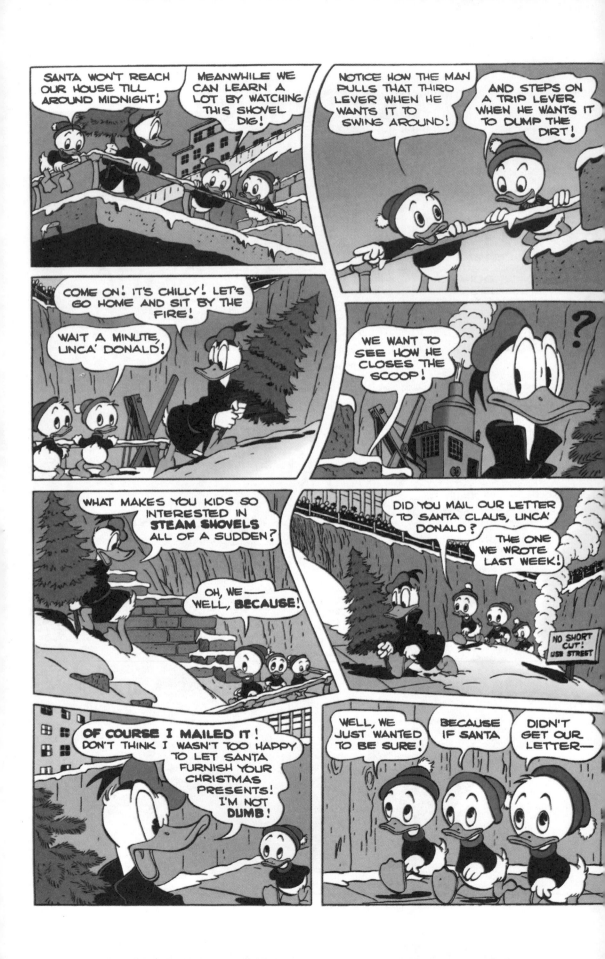

HUH?

I HAVEN'T TIME TO **ORDER** ANYTHING! I'VE GOT TO FIND A SHOVEL THAT'S MOVABLE RIGHT NOW!

LOOK LIVELY, MAN! I WANT TO BUY A STEAM SHOVEL NOW — **TONIGHT**!

ANOTHER CRACKPOT!

I JUST FINISHED TELLIN' A GUY THAT YOU **GOTTA ORDER** THEM THINGS FROM THE **FACTORY**!

WELL, WHERE'S THE FACTORY? I'LL BUY THE FACTORY!

THE SHADES OF CHRISTMAS EVE ARE DOWN BEFORE DONALD FINALLY FINDS A STEAM SHOVEL THAT IS **BUYABLE** AND **MOVABLE**!

I DON'T KNOW MUCH ABOUT HANDLING THESE THINGS, BUT WITH GOOD LUCK I'LL MAKE IT HOME!

AS HE NEARS THE INTERSECTION AT THE HEAD OF HIS HOME STREET!

THERE'S AN AWFUL RUMBLING SOUND COMING FROM THE OTHER DIRECTION!

IT'S ANOTHER STEAM SHOVEL! AND IT'S — WHY, IT'S **UNCLE SCROOGE**!

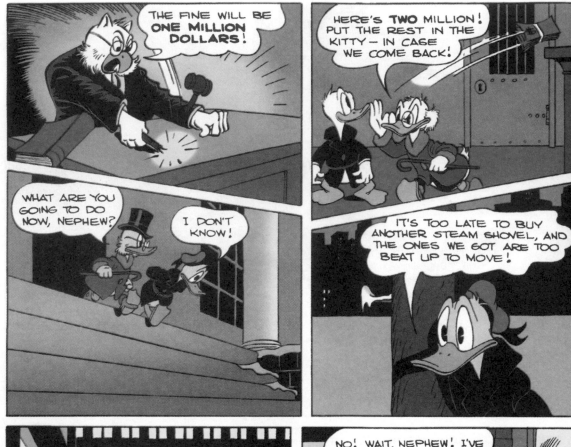

THE FINE WILL BE **ONE MILLION DOLLARS**!

HERE'S **TWO** MILLION! PUT THE REST IN THE KITTY—IN CASE WE COME BACK!

WHAT ARE YOU GOING TO DO NOW, NEPHEW?

I DON'T KNOW!

IT'S TOO LATE TO BUY ANOTHER STEAM SHOVEL, AND THE ONES WE GOT ARE TOO BEAT UP TO MOVE!

I GUESS I'LL HAVE TO TELL THE KIDS I FORGOT TO MAIL THEIR LETTER—AND **BREAK THEIR HEARTS**!

NO! WAIT, NEPHEW! I'VE BEEN AN OLD **BRAT**, BUT I'M GOING TO HELP YOU OUT OF THIS JAM!

YOU GO RENT YOURSELF A SANTA CLAUS COSTUME AND MEET ME HERE! I'LL TELL YOU THE REST OF THE SCHEME LATER!

DONALD DOESN'T KNOW HOW LUCKY HE IS TO HAVE A **BRAINY** UNCLE LIKE ME!

MEANWHILE, THE KIDS HAVE BEEN COUNTING THE HOURS, THE MINUTES, AND THE SECONDS AS THEY WAIT FOR MIDNIGHT AND SANTA CLAUS!

HALF PAST ELEVEN!

THIRTY MORE MINUTES TO WAIT!

YEAH! EIGHTEEN HUNDRED SECONDS!

I'M WORRIED ABOUT UNCA' DONALD! HE SHOULDA BEEN HOME HOURS AGO!

I'M WORRIED, TOO, BUT SANTA CLAUS IS MORE IMPORTANT!

SOME DISTANCE DOWN THE STREET!

JINGLE!

JINGLE!

TELL ME, UNCLE SCROOGE! WHAT IS THE IDEA OF THIS SCREWBALL MASQUERADE?

YOU'RE GOING TO BE SANTA CLAUS, LOUT! AND SANTA ALWAYS DRIVES UP IN A REINDEER BUGGY, DOESN'T HE?

JINGLE JINGLE

FOR HIRE

PHONE CR. 1-6157

I HEAR SLEIGH BELLS!

IT CAN'T BE SANTA!

IT'S TOO EARLY!

MAYBE THE CLOCK IS SLOW!

GET INTO THAT SANTA COSTUME AND BE READY TO GO INTO YOUR ACT!

WHAT AM I SUPPOSED TO DO?

YOU'RE GOING TO TELL THE KIDS A **HARD LUCK** STORY!

TELL 'EM YOU'RE SANTA CLAUS AND THAT YOU'RE ALL OUT OF STEAM SHOVELS THIS YEAR, BUT THAT **NEXT** CHRISTMAS —

SAY! THAT'S A **SWELL** WAY OUT OF THIS JAM! UNCLE SCROOGE, YOU'RE A **GENIUS**!

YOU'VE CALLED ME WORSE NAMES, BUT, FOR NOW, PUT ON YOUR PUTTY NOSE! WE'RE HERE!

WHOA, DONNER! WHOA, BLITZEN! WHOA, DASHER AND PRANCER!

IT **MUST** BE SANTA!

HE STOPPED IN THE ALLEY

WHERE WE CAN'T SEE HIM!

QUICK! PUT OUT THE FIRE, SO HE CAN COME **DOWN** THE CHIMNEY!

UH, OH!

THERE YOU ARE, BOYS! A TWO-TEASPOONFUL SCOOPER, WITH A ONE CANDLE-POWER FIREBOX!

OH, BOY! **EXACTLY** WHAT WE WANTED!

A **TOY** STEAM

SHOVEL!

THEY WANTED A **TOY** STEAM SHOVEL!

WHICH ANY DUMBBELL BUT **YOU** WOULD HAVE KNOWN ALL ALONG!

LOOK WHO'S TALKIN'!

AND NOW A MERRY CHRISTMAS TO YOU ALL, AND TO ALL, **GOOD NIGHT**!

SHRINNNK!

ZIP

HEY, WAIT! I'VE GOT TO SEE THAT GUY!

BOMBS AWAY!

GET OUT OF THERE! THAT MODEL AIRPLANE IS HUEY, LOUIE, AN' DEWEY'S NICEST PRESENT!

AND IF ANYTHING HAPPENS TO IT, I'LL... I'LL...

ANOTHER BOMB FOR YA, CHIP!

THANKS, DALE!

THIS TIME I'LL BE READY FOR HIM!

GOTCHA COVERED!

POP!

GRACIOUS! HE OUT OF CONTROL! HE GONNA CRASH!

CRASH

n.c.p. #2·5011 (97)

WALT DISNEY'S Donald Duck

HA! HA! GOOD OLD MISTLETOE!

THAT MUST BE DONALD NOW!

RRING!

MERRY CHRISTMAS!

COME INTO THE KITCHEN, DONALD, WHILE I FINISH THE PIES!

SURPRISE!

WHY, DONALD DUCK!

YOU HAVE TO KISS ME, DAISY!

OH, ALL RIGHT THEN — JUST ONE TEENIE WEENIE KISS!

BUT FIRST CLOSE YOUR EYES!

MICKEY MOUSE

in
Minnie's Christmas Tree.

NO, THANK YOU!

OKAY... BUT YOU'LL BE BACK!

BUT, MINNIE...

..MAYBE WE'D BETTER TAKE IT!

CERTAINLY NOT, MICKEY MOUSE! I CAN SEE IF I LISTENED TO YOU, I WOULDN'T HAVE A CENT!

AND, JUST REMEMBER, YOUR NEPHEWS ARE GOING TO BE VERY UNHAPPY WHEN THEY DON'T HAVE A TREE!

GOLLY! SHE'S RIGHT!

ALL ON ACCOUNT OF YOU...OH..! BOO-HOO -HOO-SNIFF..!

WAIT, MINNIE! I'VE GOT AN IDEA!

GOOFY AND I WILL LEAVE RIGHT AWAY FOR MY MOUNTAIN CABIN! WE'LL CUT DOWN A BEAUTY...

...AND HAVE IT BACK CHRISTMAS EVE, IN PLENTY OF TIME FOR YOU TO DECORATE IT!

WELL, YOU'D BETTER DO SOMETHING!

YEAH... I GUESS SO!

I'LL PICK UP GOOFY AND WE'LL BE OFF!

LATER...

HOW COME YOU DIDN'T BRING THUH CAR!

BECAUSE THE CAR WOULDN'T BE GOOD IN THE MOUNTAINS!

WE NEED A SLEIGH WITH ALL THIS SNOW! HURRY UP AND GET IN!

WHERE ARE THUH KIDS?

I COULDN'T TAKE 'EM ALONG THIS TIME, GOOFY! WE'VE GOT TO HURRY AND IT WOULD BE TOO TIRING A TRIP FOR THEM!

GIDDAP, TANGLEFOOT!

WE'VE GOT TO CUT A CHRISTMAS TREE FOR MINNIE!

GAWRSH! CHRISTMAS EVE IS TOMORROW NIGHT!

I KNOW...THAT'S WHY WE'VE GOT TO HURRY!

HOURS LATER... THIS MOUNTAIN AIR IS GREAT, ISN'T IT? WE'LL SLEEP LIKE LOGS TONIGHT!

YOU SAID IT!

:YAWN: I AIN'T DONE NOTHIN' BUT RIDE AN' I'M READY TUH GO TUH BED ALREADY!

WE'LL HIT THE HAY EARLY, CUT THE TREE IN THE MORNING AND BE BACK AT MINNIE'S HOUSE IN PLENTY OF TIME!

THEY'RE ALL COMING BACK IN!

THROUGH THE WINDOWS!

DOWN THE CHIMNEY!

POONK

GOOFY! WE'VE GOT TO STOP THEM **SOMEHOW**! THINK OF SOMETHING!

WHAT THE...

BONK!

WELL, OF ALL THE NERVE!

I'LL SAY...THESE GUYS'RE TOO DURNED CHUMMY!

GOOFY, IF WE'RE GOING TO GET ANY SLEEP TONIGHT, WE BETTER HOP INTO A BED FAST, WHILE IT'S STILL EMPTY...

...AND OUR NICE WOOLEN ROBE TO BOOT!

I DON'T LOSE MUH TEMPER OFTEN...BUT I'M GOIN' TUH PULL 'EM ALL OUTA THERE!

STOP IT, GOOFY! WE'RE NOT GOING TO MESS WITH BEARS AGAIN!

WE'LL RIDE BACK ON TANGLEFOOT! HE DOESN'T MIND CARRYING TWO OF US!

GIVE US ALL THE SPEED YOU'VE GOT, TANGLEFOOT... WE'VE GOT A LONG WAY TO GO!

I HOPE THAT FELLER HAS A TREE LEFT!

CHRISTMAS EVE AT THE TREE LOT!

HELLO, SON! I KNEW YOU'D BE BACK SOONER OR LATER! YOU'RE LUCKY, TOO...I'VE GOT ONE TREE LEFT!

WHOA, TANGLEFOOT!

YOU DON'T MEAN TO TELL ME THIS IS ALL YOU HAVE?

THAT'S RIGHT, SON!

...AND, SEEIN' HOW IT'S MY LAST TREE, I'LL LET IT GO FOR A DOLLAR AN INCH...THAT'S ONLY TWENTY DOLLARS!

TWENTY DOLLARS FOR THIS?

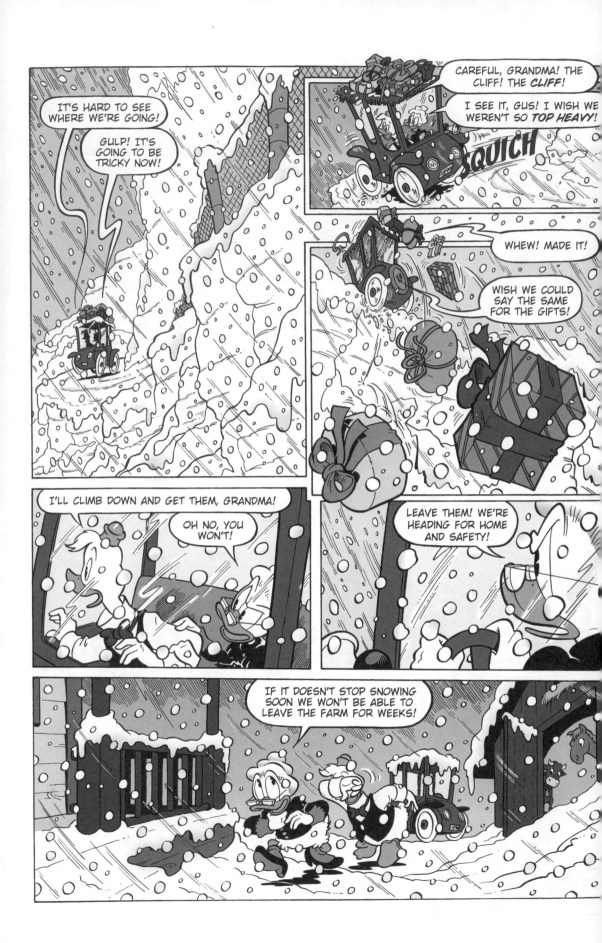

DOES THAT MEAN WE'LL HAVE TO *CANCEL* CHRISTMAS?

WE CAN'T DO ANY MORE CHRISTMAS SHOPPING, THAT'S FOR SURE!

I CAN'T GO THROUGH ALL THAT AGAIN! BESIDES, THOSE GIFTS I BOUGHT WERE EXTRA SPECIAL!

SO WHAT'LL WE DO?

WE'LL *MAKE* OUR OWN PRESENTS! JUST LIKE WE USED TO IN THE *GOOD OLD DAYS!*

...ATER...

DAISY'LL LOVE THIS SWEATER...IN FACT I WOULDN'T MIND IT MYSELF!

THESE ARE DONALD'S FAVORITE COOKIES...HARD TO THINK OF HAVING TO WAIT UNTIL CHRISTMAS DAY TO EAT THEM!

AND I'VE GOTTA MAKE SOMETHING FESTIVE TINS FOR THE COOKIES TO GO IN! THERE!

GRANDMA! COME AND SEE THE GIFT I MADE FOR THE BOYS!

NEXT MORNING--

THIS IS GETTING RIDICULOUS! *MORE* SNOW! IT'S LIKE SOMEBODY ASKED A GENIE FOR A RECORD-BREAKING WINTER!

I WONDER HOW MY SALTED BACK GARDEN WEATHERED THE STORM?

JUMPING JINGLE-BELLS! AM I *DELIRIOUS* FROM *SNOW-FEVER?*

HEY, MICKEY! LOOKS LIKE ANOTHER *SCORCHER!*

IS THAT COAT SOME KIND OF *GAG?* BETTER BE CAREFUL, OR YOU'LL GET HEAT PROSTRATION IN THIS WARM WEATHER!

BUT THERE WAS JUST A *SNOWSTORM!*

MAYBE IN YOUR *DREAMS--* BUT NOT IN REALITY! THIS IS THE MIDDLE OF JULY!

I'LL BE RIGHT BACK!

MAYBE IT'S SOME KIND OF *FLUKE* WEATHER PATTERN! I'VE GOTTA SEE IF IT'S JUST AS WARM IN MINNIE'S NEIGHBORHOOD--

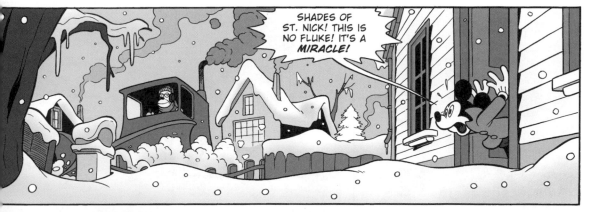

SHADES OF ST. NICK! THIS IS NO FLUKE! IT'S A *MIRACLE!*

WHAT DID SHE SAY ABOUT IT BEING JULY?

JULY 14TH, 2001 TO BE EXACT! WHY? MISS SOMEONE'S BIRTHDAY?

MISS A...A *BIRTHDAY?*

IT LOOKS LIKE I'VE *GAINED A PATH* TO THE *PAST!*

MY HOUSE HAS BECOME THE CENTER OF SOME MYSTERIOUS *TEMPORAL VORTEX!*

OH, MICKEY! IS THIS ONE OF YOUR *JOKES?!*

Y' SURE ARE A *KIDDER,* MICKEY!

SOMETIMES WE *ALL* THINK WE'RE THE CENTER OF THINGS!

PLEASE DON'T TELL CLARABELLE I ATE HER CHOCOLATE!

A *CORTEX?* AIN'T THAT PART O' THUH *EYE?*

WELL, MAYBE MY FRIENDS DON'T GET THE IMPLICATIONS! BUT *I* DO!

AND I'M GOING TO TAKE **ADVANTAGE** OF THIS LITTLE MYSTERY!

WHY YES, WE **DO** STILL HAVE SOME CHRISTMAS WRAP! DOING YOUR CHRISTMAS SHOPPING **EARLY** THIS YEAR?

MISTER--FROM **MY** POINT OF VIEW, IT'S **JUST IN TIME!**

WELL, THAT'S HALF MY SHOPPING DONE... BUT THIS WHOLE **MYSTERY** IS **NAGGING** ME!

WHAT'S GOING ON? **WHY?**

I KNOW HOW TO FIND OUT! I'LL ASK **DOC STATIC** TO GET TOGETHER SOME OF HIS SCIENTIFIC ASSOCIATES!

MICKEY, THANKS **SO** MUCH FOR SHARING THIS! MY COLLEAGUES ARE **ALREADY** FULL OF THEORIES, BUT WE'RE **DYING** TO EXAMINE THE PHENOMENON FIRST HAND!

WHEN YOU JUMP BACK TO "JULY-WORLD", YOU CAN'T MEET YOUR PAST SELF THERE! EITHER YOU EXIST "NOW", OR YOU EXIST LAST JULY!

DOC STATIC

WE PLAN TO SET UP ONE RELAY IN WINTER, AND A SECOND IN SUMMER, THEN *MEASURE* THE *DISTANCE BETWEEN* THEM!

TO DETERMINE IF SPACE IS AFFECTED AS WELL AS TIME!

SOUNDS GOOD! JUST EXPLAIN IT TO ME WHEN YOU'RE DONE--

HUH-- *HORACE!*

REVISIT LAST SUMMER- ONLY $20

STEP RIGHT UP, FOLKS! *LOSE* THAT WINTER CHILL! FOR A *SLIGHT* FEE YOU CAN CATCH UP ON YOUR CHRISTMAS SHOPPING, VISIT THE *BEACH,* AND EVEN GET *SWEATY!*

HEY, MICK! I THOUGHT YOU WERE *JOKING--* UNTIL I WENT THROUGH YOUR HOUSE INTO THE PAST TO BUY MORE CHOCOLATE!

I'M MAKING A *FORTUNE!* AND YOU'LL GET YOUR CUT WHEN THE TIME COMES!

MICKEY, WE'D LIKE TO GET STARTED!

CERTAINLY! TWENTY DOLLARS APIECE, GENTLEMEN!

HEY! THEY'RE HERE AT *MY* INVITATION! YOU CAN'T *CHARGE* THEM!

BUT THIS IS A *ONCE-IN-A-LIFETIME* OPPORTUNITY! YOU WANT US TO LET PEOPLE INTO YOUR HOUSE FOR *FREE?!*

WE'LL MAKE MONEY *LATER*, HORACE! BETTER LET DOC'S CREW THROUGH BEFORE THEY *COMPLAIN* TO THOSE *PRESS PEOPLE* AND *COPS*!

~:GULP!:~ YOU THINK...

YOU WITH THE MEGAPHONE! TELL US ABOUT YOUR *AMAZING ENTERPRISE* HERE!

HEY! *SURE!*

~:OOMF!:~

GET IN LINE, PAL!

~:GROAN!:~ NOW *I'VE* GOTTA ENLIST THE POLICE... TO CLEAR THOSE YELLOW *JOURNALISTS* AWAY!

ONE SIDE, CITIZEN! I WANT TO SEE *JULY!*

~:OOMF!:~

I'M AFRAID YOU'LL HAVE TO *WAIT* YOUR TURN AT THE END OF THE *LINE!*

BUT THIS IS *MY HOUSE!* AND I GOTTA TALK TO HORACE, SO--

HEY! WILL *SOMEBODY* LET ME THROUGH? *PLEASE?*

⇥OOMF!⇤ THIS IS GETTING *REPETITIVE!*

OH, WELL! IF YOU CAN'T BEAT 'EM, JOIN 'EM! I *DO* HAVE MORE CHRISTMAS GIFTS TO BUY...

...SO IF I CAN'T GET TO HORACE FOR NOW, I'LL USE MY *SIDE-DOOR KEY* TO GO BACK TO THE *SUMMER* AND *SHOP!*

⇥WHEW!⇤ LOOK AT THESE *CROWDS!* BACK HERE SHOPPING IN JULY ALONG WITH ME!

EMPORIUM

WE'RE *ALL SOLD OUT!* ⇥HEE-HEE!⇤ IT'S LIKE *CHRISTMAS IN JULY!*

VISIONS OF SUGARPLUMS! OF *COURSE* IT IS!

ALL SOLD OUT!

ALL THOSE SHOPPERS ARE FROM THE *FUTURE,* WHEN IT *IS* ALMOST CHRISTMAS!

WELL, I GOT MY SHOPPING FINISHED! BUT NEXT TIME A TEMPORAL ANOMALY HAPPENS IN MY HOUSE, I'M KEEPING IT TO MYSELF!

WITH ANY LUCK, THINGS WILL BE CALMER WHEN I HEAD BACK TO THE *PRESENT* WITH MY *PRESENTS!* HO, HO, H--

DONNER AND BLITZEN! THAT'S *MUSCLES MCGURK*... COLLECTING SOME KIND OF *EXTRA* PAYMENT!

BUT THERE WAS NO *RETURN FEE* WHEN I *LEFT!*

THERE IS *NOW!* AND IT'S NO USE TRYING TO GET IN THROUGH THE SIDE DOOR... *HORACE* HAD ME *BOARD IT UP!*

BACK TO WINTER SPECIAL! ONLY $10

AND I SPENT ALL MY CASH ON GIFTS! WELL, HORACE MUSTA GIVEN MUSCLES WORD TO LET *ME* IN FOR FREE!

HEY, MUSCLES! HORACE MUST HAVE SAID *I* COULD COME THROUGH FOR FREE! RIGHT?

YEAH-- *RIGHT!* AND I'M SANTA CLAUS!

⇒SIGH!⇐ I CAN SEE THROUGH TO WINTER! THERE'S HORACE IN A LIMO, THE BUM--*ENJOYING* THE *MONEY* HE'S MAKING OFF *MY* HOME! THIS MIRACLE HAS TURNED INTO A CURSE!

WILL I *EVER* MAKE IT BACK TO CHRISTMASTIME? OR DO I JUST HAVE TO LIVE THROUGH THE NEXT SIX MONTHS... *AGAIN?*

IF ONLY THERE WAS SOME OTHER WAY TO GET INTO MY HOUSE AND EXIT THROUGH THE FRONT DOOR!

MAYBE IF I JUST RUN AROUND THE OUTSIDE, *WITHOUT* GOING THROUGH ANY DOOR, THE SEASONS MIGHT SOMEHOW *CHANGE AGAIN--*

⇥SIGH!⇤

TIME TRAPS AND VORTEX TRICKS! *I JUST WISH THINGS WOULD GO BACK TO NORMAL!*

POOF!

⇥HUH?!⇤ THEY *DID!* IT'S *WINTER* AGAIN--

WHAT THE HECK IS *GOING ON* HERE?

HEY! WHERE'S MY LIMO?

I'LL TELL YOU...IT'S *ME!*

-*GASP!*-

I'M A RECENTLY LICENSED *ROCK-SALT ELF!* IT'S MY *JOB* TO *MAGICALLY TEACH PEOPLE LESSONS!*

YOU *WISHED* YOU COULD SWITCH BACK AND FORTH BETWEEN WINTER AND SUMMER WEATHER! IT WAS MY *DUTY* TO PROVE THAT WAS A *BAD IDEA!*

I JUST HOPE YOU LEARNED YOUR *LESSON!*

WHAT ARE YOU *TALKING* ABOUT?

ALL I *ASKED* FOR WAS A LITTLE WARM WEATHER! MY *HOUSE* WAS TAKEN OVER AND YOUR *MAGIC* CAUSED *CHAOS!* I DIDN'T LEARN *ANYTHING!*

YOU KNOW, YOU'VE GOT A POINT THERE! I'M SORRY, PAL...I *AM* KIND OF *NEW* AT THIS MAGIC STUFF!

HOLD STILL, YOU MAGICAL *MONKEY-WRENCH!*

GEE, MAYBE I SHOULD FIND ANOTHER JOB!

ONE ROAD TRIP INTO THE MOUNTAINS LATER—

HERE WE ARE! OUR HOLIDAY GETAWAY! AND THE RENT ON THIS CABIN WAS DOWNRIGHT CHEAP!

NO WONDER! A PLACE LIKE THIS IS MEANT FOR SPENDING SUMMER VACATIONS IN THE WARM SUNSHINE!

TAA-DAA! A SIMPLE DOMICILE EXACTLY LIKE OUR FORE-FATHERS HAD! WHAT DO YOU THINK?

DID THOSE FOREFATHERS LIVE IN A MUSTY TOOL SHED?

CAN THE WISE-LIPS, BOYS! SOME STOCKINGS HUNG BY THE CHIMNEY OUGHTA PUT US IN THE MOOD!

YEAH! THE MOOD TO GO BACK HOME!

THERE'S NOTHING TO DO HERE! WE'RE BORED!

AND COLD!

AND HUNGRY!

WE'LL FIX THAT! LET'S GET THIS OL' STOVE LIT AND...

HMM! KINDLING'S NOT CATCHING! MAYBE I SHOULD BLOW ON THE FLAME!

WHOOOSH!

OH WELL! WHO NEEDS A STOVE?! WE'LL EAT STRAIGHT OUT OF THE CAN!

COLD BEANS? THIS IS THE ESSENCE OF CHRISTMAS?

SURE! THEN WE'LL HAVE A MUG OF FREEZING CIDER IN FRONT OF A NON-EXISTANT FIRE!

A BEAR! RIGHT IN MY CABIN! THAT'S JUST MY LUCK!

WELL, I CAN'T STAY ON THE ROOF ALL NIGHT! I'VE GOTTA SHOW THAT RAMPAGING BEAST WHO'S BOSS!

ALL RIGHT, YOU SEETHING MASS OF MUSCLES AND FANGS! I'M COMING! DO YOUR WORST!

HEY! C'MON! WAKE UP, BONGO, AND BEAT IT! AMSCRAY!

ZZZZZ ZZZZZZZ!

I DON'T *BELIEVE* IT! THIS MANGY MONSTER'S OUT LIKE A LIGHT! HE MUST BE HIBERNATING!

CLANG!

CLANG!

THIS IS HOW OUR FOREFATHERS DEALT WITH DEADLY DANGER! *WHEEZE!* BUT I CAN'T JUST LEAVE THE POOR THING OUT IN THE COLD!

THERE! THAT OUGHTA HOLD THE NARCOLEPTIC LUNK TILL THE SPRING THAW!

ZZZZZZ!

JEEZ! I'M *FREEZING!* BETTER GET A FIRE GOING IN THE CABIN WHILE I WAIT FOR THE BUH- BUH-BOYS TO SHOW!

YIPPIE! WE HAVE THE TOYS OF OUR DREAMS!

THEY'RE FILLED TO TO THE BRIM AND READY FOR ACTION!

HOLD THE PHONE! UNCA DONALD SAID NO TOYS ON THIS TRIP! HE'LL PITCH A FIT IF HE FINDS OUT WE BOUGHT THE DRENCHER-SOAKERS!

BUT DONALD HAS OTHER PROBLEMS—

BRRR! THE WOOD IN THIS FIREPLACE WON'T LIGHT! IT'S USELESS! RATS!

WELL, FORGET THOSE RUSTIC FOREFATHERS! MAYBE THEY NEVER SOAKED THEIR LOGS IN LIGHTER FLUID, BUT I WILL!

SQUIRT!

I KNOW! WE'LL BURY THE DRENCHER-SOAKERS IN THE SNOW...

...THEN DIG 'EM UP LATER AND SNEAK 'EM INTO THE CAR WHEN IT'S TIME TO LEAVE THE MOUNTAINS!

UNCA DONALD WILL NEVER KNOW WE HAVE THEM!

SPEAKING OF UNCA DONALD, I'LL BET HE'S GOT A WARM, COZY BLAZE GOING IN THE CABIN RIGHT NOW!

OR, NOT YET—

OKEE-DOKE! THE LOGS ARE SOAKED! LET'S GET THINGS TOASTY AROUND HERE!

YOICKS!

WHAWOOOM!